What Was Woodstock?

by Joan Holub

illustrated by Gregory Copeland

Grosset & Dunlap
An Imprint of Penguin Random House

GROSSET & DUNLAP
Penguin Young Readers Group
An Imprint of Penguin Random House LLC

Text copyright © 2016 by Joan Holub. Illustrations copyright © 2016 by Penguin
Random House LLC. All rights reserved. Published by Grosset & Dunlap, an imprint
of Penguin Random House LLC, 345 Hudson Street, New York, New York 10014.
GROSSET & DUNLAP is a trademark of Penguin Random House LLC.
Printed in the USA.

Library of Congress Cataloging-in-Publication Data is available.

ISBN 978-0-448-48696-3   10 9 8 7 6 5 4 3 2 1

Contents

What Was Woodstock?

Woodstock was an outdoor rock festival in a small New York town. It took place over three days in August of 1969. Doesn't sound like anything so special, does it? Yet, today, so many years later, Woodstock has become part of the history of the 1960s.

About fifty thousand people were expected to come. Surprise! Ten times that many showed up—almost half a million people! No concert had ever attracted so many fans. Thirty-two of the hottest rock and folk bands performed onstage. It was a happening—hippie slang for a super-exciting event for cool people.

Woodstock could have been a disaster. The four guys in charge hardly had any experience planning a festival. And a lot did go wrong.

Traffic jams for miles around blocked the way to the concert. It rained during the performances, and the electricity went out. There was not nearly enough food or water for the crowd. There weren't enough bathrooms.

Sounds terrible, doesn't it? As the festival began, TV and newspapers reported that it was a great big mess. Families panicked. Were their teenagers who'd gone to Woodstock safe? Some people wanted to send in soldiers to stop the festival before it really got started. They expected riots that weekend at Woodstock.

Many thought the festival would be a flop.

It wasn't. It was exactly the opposite. It was out of sight, which in the 1960s meant awesome.

The crowd at Woodstock thought the music was amazing. Many of the musicians were wowed by the good-natured crowd, too. And nearby townspeople were surprised to discover that the young fans were mostly nice and polite.

The year 1969 was an unhappy time in the United States. Many young people were angry about a far-off war in Southeast Asia. They felt misunderstood and ignored. They were looking for peace, love, and freedom. For three days, that's what they found at Woodstock.

CHAPTER 1
A Concert

It was the 1960s. Hip musicians like Bob Dylan were moving to Woodstock, New York. It was a pretty town with trees and farmland, about 120 miles north of New York City.

NY

Buffalo Woodstock ☆

Boston

Pittsburgh

New York City

Philadelphia

Baltimore

A twenty-four-year-old music promoter named Michael Lang got an idea. Maybe he should build a recording studio in Woodstock. Musicians from nearby could record their songs in his studio instead of driving all the way into New York City. And running a studio would be fun!

Lang was a hippie with big ideas and confidence. Although a bit shy, he was good at talking people into things. He tried to get someone to invest money in his recording studio.

In November 1968 he met Artie Kornfeld. Kornfeld was a vice president at Capitol Records. He wasn't sold on Lang's idea. Also, he didn't have enough money for the project. But Kornfeld knew lots of bands and people in the music industry. The two men ended up hanging out together and became friends.

While playing pool, they came up with a new idea. Wouldn't it be groovy to have a big outdoor concert in Woodstock? They could sell tickets and use the money to pay for building a recording studio!

In February 1969, Lang and Kornfeld met two businessmen named Joel Rosenman and John Roberts. They were willing to invest—put money of their own—in cool ideas.

Rosenman and Roberts didn't know much about hippies like Lang and Kornfeld. They had already invested in building a recording studio in New York City. So they weren't interested in the idea of another studio. Not at first. But then Lang and Kornfeld mentioned their Woodstock concert idea. That caught the businessmen's attention. A big concert could be a moneymaker and would be great promotion for the recording studio before it was even built.

Rosenman and Roberts thought it over. They were in! The four men—all in their twenties—formed a company called Woodstock Ventures Incorporated. Their event would be called the Woodstock Music and Art Fair. Soon people would begin calling it the "Woodstock Festival" or simply "Woodstock," for short.

Planning started for a concert with an audience of fifty thousand. The date was set for August 15–17. First off, they needed to pick an outdoor site. Locations in the town of Woodstock turned out to be too small. They went looking for a bigger site in towns nearby. They wanted someplace pretty, with grass and trees.

They would also need security guards, toilets, food, water, a stage, and lighting. And, oh yeah, music! Bands had to be hired. Their hope was that all the top singers and groups would sign contracts to play at their festival. A timeline and to-do lists were made. It was a lot to organize.

The team of four started out with high spirits, high hopes, and big plans. They just knew their concert was going to be outta sight!

Hippies

The hippie movement began in the 1960s.
The word comes from "hip" as in "cool." Most
hippies were in their teens and twenties
and came from ordinary families. Hippies
were all about peace and love, and
were against war. They rejected
many of their parents' ways,
beliefs, and music.

long hair

choker

tie-dyed T-shirt

vest

bellbottom,
hip-hugger jeans

sandals

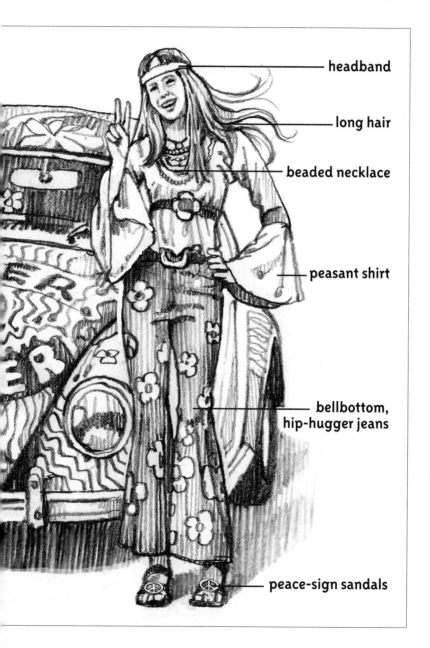

headband

long hair

beaded necklace

peasant shirt

bellbottom,
hip-hugger jeans

peace-sign sandals

11

CHAPTER 2
Yasgur's Farm

Woodstock Ventures only had about five months to make the concert happen. They needed everything—fast. That meant they had to pay high prices. Of course, they hoped to earn all their expenses back. They'd make money selling concert tickets. Plus, they planned to make a film and album based on their festival.

They picked a site in Wallkill, New York, about forty miles south of Woodstock. They had a meeting with some town leaders. It seemed they would approve the idea of having a festival there. So a building crew began work.

Over the following weeks, some Wallkill residents grew worried. They wanted to stop the festival. It would be noisy. They'd heard that hippies were dirty, rude, and violent. And hippies were known for using illegal drugs like marijuana, which was nicknamed weed, pot, or grass.

The Woodstock producers argued with the town. They'd already spent time and money working in Wallkill. But in mid-July, the town officially turned them away. There was only one month left till the concert! It wasn't much time to start over from scratch.

Tens of thousands of tickets had already been sold. If you bought tickets early by mail or in a record store, they were cheaper. They cost eighteen dollars for all three days, thirteen dollars for two days, or seven dollars for one day. (Tickets were going to

be twenty-four dollars on festival weekend.)

If they had to cancel the concert, the Woodstock team would have to give all that money back. And they'd lose all they'd spent so far in advertising, planning, and building. Did they give up? No! They looked for a new festival site—fast.

Michael Lang took a helicopter ride around the area. The first place he visited turned out to be a swamp. Then someone told him about a farm in Bethel, New York.

Lang and Mel Lawrence went to check it out. Lawrence was director of operations. That meant he was in charge of building, landscaping, and coordinating many details of the event. The two guys drove down a street called Happy Avenue on the way to the farm. Happy Avenue? That seemed like a good sign. It turned out that the site had a sloping hillside shaped like a giant shallow bowl. It was more than big enough to seat the expected crowd. At the bottom of the hill there was a flat area where the stage could go. It would be like stadium seating. Everyone would have a good view of the bands onstage.

Yasgur's Farm

Lang started getting excited. He asked to lease about six hundred acres of field. Unfortunately, the owners, Max and Miriam Yasgur, said no. They were dairy farmers and were growing a crop of alfalfa there to feed their cows.

Lang was desperate. He told Max Yasgur what had happened in Wallkill. Yasgur agreed that hadn't been fair. He was almost fifty years old and didn't know much about hippies. However, he thought all young people deserved a chance to show they could be well-behaved. He agreed to lease the property to Woodstock Ventures. But they had to guarantee to leave his farm in good shape after the festival. A deal was made.

On July 22, only one week after the Wallkill site fell through, the festival's building crew moved to Yasgur's farm.

Max Yasgur (1919–1973)

Max and Miriam Yasgur owned many acres of farmland in Bethel, New York. They worked hard to make their dairy business successful. People in town respected and trusted Max. He was an honest guy who often helped set things right when there were arguments in the town. Since he was on the festival's side, it helped convince some of his neighbors that everything would be okay. Others didn't want the event to happen. They posted protest signs that said, "Stop Max's Hippy Music Festival."

CHAPTER 3
Getting Ready

Bethel was about sixty-five miles from Woodstock. Still, Lang and his partners decided to keep their original festival name, the Woodstock Music and Art Fair. The word "Woodstock" sounded outdoorsy and peaceful, which was the vibe, or mood, they wanted.

They advertised the festival on the radio and in newspapers. Kornfeld knew some hippie news reporters and got them to stir up interest in the festival. But the producers wanted more than just hippies to come. Their advertising was directed at all people in their teens and twenties. This was the generation known as "baby boomers." After World War II ended in 1945, there had been a big boom—increase—in the number of babies born. The oldest baby boomers were about twenty-three years old in 1969.

Two different posters promoted the festival. One of them became famous. An artist named Arnold Skolnick created it. It was simple, with a white peace dove sitting on a guitar neck, framed

by a red background. The dove symbolized peace. And the guitar symbolized music. The poster's tagline read, "3 Days of Peace & Music." That was what the four promoters wanted their outdoor concert to be. Later the artist said the dove was really a catbird. Still, his design became a popular symbol of the festival.

Peace Symbol

In the 1950s, Gerald Holtom designed the peace symbol in England. He and others were against the use of nuclear bombs. The peace symbol was based on a system of sending messages with flag signals. It combined the flag signals for *N* and *D*. *ND* stood for *nuclear disarmament*, which meant getting rid of all atomic and hydrogen bombs. In 1960, a college student brought peace-symbol badges from England to the United States. Soon the symbol was used in US antiwar protests, too.

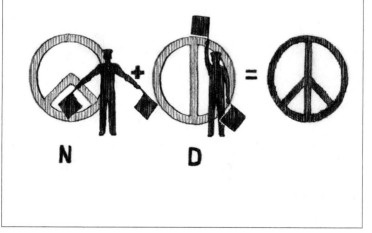

N   D

The first posters printed didn't list the groups who would play at Woodstock. But there were rumors. Maybe the Beatles would come!

The Beatles

They were the most popular rock group ever. However, the Fab Four—John, Paul, George, and Ringo—were breaking up. So they didn't come to Woodstock. Others musicians who said no included the Doors, Jethro Tull, Led Zeppelin, the Moody Blues, and Bob Dylan.

In fact, at first not a single band said yes. Popular groups got high-paying gigs. Why should they take a chance on a festival with an uncertain future? Lang's partners grew worried when musicians kept saying no, but he played it cool.

In mid-April, one of the hottest rock bands around finally said yes. It was Creedence Clearwater Revival. Their "Proud Mary" and "Bad Moon Rising" were hits in 1969. Their concerts were always sold out.

Creedence Clearwater Revival

The Woodstock producers were overjoyed. When other bands heard that Creedence signed on to play, they suddenly got interested, too. The highest-paid performer to play Woodstock would be Jimi Hendrix. He got $18,000. Back then, that was enough to buy six new cars.

Jimi Hendrix

Woodstock Ventures set up an office trailer on Yasgur's land. There was so much to do! Was there really enough time to pull off such a big event? Sometimes crews worked twenty hours a day, building a stage and sound towers, running electric cables, and setting up the lighting.

Off-duty New York police officers were hired as security for the festival. They had to have an interview first. Woodstock Venture's hippie workers watched the policemen closely. Did they frown at hippie clothes or long hair? Were they grumpy? Policemen like that weren't chosen. The festival team was looking for a friendly security staff who could handle things peacefully.

Weapons weren't allowed at the festival—not even for the police. No guns, no sticks, no handcuffs. Security teams would have to keep the peace with calmness, kindness, and understanding.

And cream pies!

A hippie commune called the Hog Farm was hired to set up the campground. They ended up helping with security and providing free food, too. (A commune is a group of people who live and work together and share everything equally.) Sometimes the Hog Farmers acted like clowns, turning anger to laughter by tossing gooey pies at people. Some had funny nicknames like Wavy Gravy and Muskrat.

Vietnam War

In the 1960s, the United States was fighting a war far off in Southeast Asia. It wanted to keep communist North Vietnam from taking over non-communist South Vietnam. In communist countries, there is no democracy. There is only one political party and little freedom. Many in the United States were scared that communism might take over the world.

At the time of the festival, men could be drafted into the army beginning at age eighteen. It meant that you had to be a soldier even if you didn't want to. Yet young men could not vote to decide about war or anything else until age twenty-one. Many thought this was unfair. Some protested against the government. Other Americans believed such protests were unpatriotic. In 1969, half a million US soldiers were involved in the Vietnam War. That's about the same number of people that went to Woodstock. In 1971, the voting age in America was lowered to eighteen. US combat troops finally left Vietnam in 1973. By that time, over three million Vietnamese and 58,000 Americans had died.

Just days before the festival, good news came. Woodstock Ventures got a film deal. Warner Bros. would pay the costs of making a documentary film of the concert. The profits would be split between the film company and the festival producers. A young director named Michael Wadleigh would capture the concert on film. One of his crew members would be Martin Scorsese. He became a famous director of many films including *Raging Bull* and *Hugo*.

Michael Wadleigh

CHAPTER 4
Early Birds

The Wednesday before the festival began, crews were still building the stage and sound towers. Yet about fifty thousand fans had already arrived! The advertising had worked. Maybe too well. News about the festival had spread far and wide. By Friday morning, 175,000 people had come. However, it looked like many more than that were on the way.

Could the festival handle such a huge crowd?

People who lived along the roads to the festival sat on lawn chairs in their front yards. They watched a parade of thousands of hippies and other young people drive by. Many were in wildly painted busses or vans, and cars with painted slogans like "Woodstock or Bust." Soon there were so many cars headed for the festival that traffic creeped along. Then it completely stopped! Drivers gave up and parked their cars along the side of the road, in parking lots, cemeteries, or anywhere there was space. Then crowds of music fans walked ten miles or more to Yasgur's farm. It was the only way to get there now.

The fans' excitement grew as they approached the concert area. Then they got confused. There were no ticket booths set up yet. No one knew where to buy tickets or to hand in the tickets they'd bought in advance.

Things quickly spun out of control. The fence around the concert area wasn't finished. Fans could just enter. There wasn't enough security to stop them. So there was no way to make sure everyone paid. The festival organizers came to a quick decision. All parts of the fence were taken down.

Woodstock was declared a free concert! Anybody who showed up was welcome. This was great for fans, but a disaster for the organizers. They'd overspent. Without more tickets sales, how would they pay the bills?

Once on the farm's hillside, fans chose good spots. They claimed them by spreading blankets, setting out belongings, or leaving a friend in charge. Then they walked around, meeting people, looking for snacks, or hoping to see musicians.

The Hog Farmers tried to entertain the crowd. They led yoga exercises from the stage. Thousands of fans on the hillside joined in, taking deep breaths and stretching their muscles. Hog Farmers believed in living simply and knew how to do things to survive outdoors. In the nearby campgrounds, they helped people set up tents or tarps for sleeping. They showed them how to build cooking fires.

People in the crowd quickly made friends and shared the excitement of being together. "Where are you from?" they'd ask one another. It turned out, they'd come to Woodstock from as far away as California, Washington, Florida, and Alabama. And they had a lot in common. They wanted peace, not war. Instead of hello or good-bye, they often said, "Peace, man." They'd flash a peace sign—two fingers held up in a *V*.

War wasn't the only thing on their minds, though. Mostly, they'd come to Woodstock for fun and music. Those who arrived early found

ways to have fun before the music even began. They went swimming or skinny-dipping in the nearby lakes. There was a playground area with a wooden jungle gym. It was meant for the little kids at the festival, but older fans played there, too. Long, sturdy vines had been hung from the trees. People swung out on them, let go, and landed in piles of hay. They danced, strummed guitars, and explored the area.

Meanwhile, traffic leading to the concert got worse. Authorities worried about such a huge crowd. It could easily turn into an angry mob. There could be riots! The National Guard— government soldiers—was all set to go in and remove everyone from Yasgur's land. Woodstock Ventures said there was no need for that. So the National Guard was called off. However, hundreds of local sheriffs, state troopers, and volunteer police needed to help out with traffic and crowd control before the weekend was out.

The 1960s

The 1960s was a decade of social and political change. Civil rights was a hot issue. African Americans, Mexican Americans, Native Americans, women, and gays and lesbians were demanding fair treatment. There were sit-ins, freedom rides, protest marches, and even riots. Students protested the Vietnam War. There was tragedy. Four important leaders were killed: President John F. Kennedy, civil rights leaders Martin Luther King Jr. and Malcolm X, and Senator Robert F. Kennedy. Americans were devastated and angered by these losses. The 1960s was one of the most upsetting and—at the same time—exciting decades ever in America.

CHAPTER 5
Friday

The plan was to have folk music on Friday. That would start things off in a mellow way. Wild rock and roll would begin Saturday. At seven on Friday morning, Michael Lang realized there was no one to introduce bands and make announcements onstage. Chip Monck was in charge of stage lighting and technical design, but he also got the job master of ceremonies on the spot. He turned out to be great at it.

Around noon, the sound system was checked. Everything was working fine . . . except no bands had arrived! The producers needed to give the kids what they'd come for. Music! And fast.

Music was supposed to start at four that afternoon. The first band on the program was

Sweetwater. But they were caught in traffic. Other bands were stuck at hotels seven miles away. Cars were no use. Helicopters had to be found.

The crowd was getting bored and restless. Tens of thousands of fans had already been there for days, waiting. They covered the enormous hillside, all staring at the stage. It was hot, in the nineties. As time passed, the festival staff began to panic. Recently, at smaller concerts, fights had broken out. No one wanted that to happen at Woodstock.

Richie Havens

Richie Havens, a folk-rock singer, was flown in from one of the hotels. He was supposed to play later in the day but agreed to go on early. This was brave. No one had ever played for a crowd this big. Were people in a bad mood because of the delay? Were they in a troublemaking mood?

At five o'clock that afternoon Havens stepped onstage wearing an orange African-style shirt called a dashiki. He became famous as the first performer to play Woodstock! After four songs, he thought he was finished. But festival organizers kept sending him back for more. Eventually he ran out of songs. So he made up one based on a gospel song and called it "Freedom." It got people clapping and started things off on the right note.

Then to fill more time, a Hindu spiritual leader from India came up onstage to bless the festival. He told fans that Woodstock would be a time of peace and love. A calming, happy vibe filled the crowd.

Singer Country Joe McDonald wasn't supposed to play until Sunday. Festival organizers found him backstage and begged him to play right then. He said no way. He didn't even have his guitar with him. No problem! Someone borrowed a guitar and gave him a rope for a strap so he could hang it around his neck. In minutes, he was onstage. Country Joe was known for being against the Vietnam War. He began by leading the crowd in a rousing cheer. Then he sang a bouncy antiwar song called "Fixin to Die Rag," and fans sang along with him.

But who would come on after Country Joe? Backstage, promoters looked for a band to follow him. They found John Sebastian from the Lovin' Spoonful. He wasn't supposed to play at the festival at all. He'd only come to hang out with friends. Luckily, he had brought his guitar. And he'd recently written some brand-new songs. Would he play them? To help out, he did.

He couldn't remember all the words to the new songs, but the crowd didn't mind. They were excited!

Joe McDonald

Finally, Sweetwater arrived by helicopter. The concert was back on track!

Already Woodstock was making history. That night, a festival coordinator named John Morris made an announcement. Standing onstage at the microphone, he told the kids they were the biggest crowd to ever come together. He thought it was too bad they couldn't see each other in the dark. So he made a suggestion: "I want every one of you to light a match." Instantly, thousands of tiny lights flickered on in the blackness all across the hillside. A sense of togetherness and wonder swept the crowd. It was a magical moment.

Two folk megastars had been saved for last. Arlo Guthrie was only eighteen but was already legendary. Joan Baez followed around 1:00 a.m.

Arlo Guthrie

She closed with a spiritual, "Swing Low, Sweet Chariot," and the powerful protest song "We Shall Overcome."

Joan Baez

After the show ended for the night, some fans
went to their tents in nearby campgrounds. Most
people just stayed on the hill. They went to sleep
on their jackets, on the damp ground, or by using
a neighbor's knees as pillows.

By now, almost five hundred thousand people
were crowded into the concert area. If the festival
had been a city, it would've been the third largest
in New York! The audience was so big, it would
later be nicknamed Woodstock Nation.

And still people kept coming. Cars were backed up almost twenty miles. An estimated two hundred fifty thousand more people tried to get to Woodstock but were turned away.

Meanwhile, Michael Wadleigh and his crew were there capturing everything on film—the crowd, the traffic, the mess, and the music!

Sixties Slang

Bread—money

Bummed out—unhappy

Bummer—unhappy experience

Flip out—get upset

Flower child—hippie

Flower power—a peace slogan

Freak out—get upset

Groovy, far out, cool, outta sight—great

A happening—an important, exciting event

Hassle—trouble

It'll blow you away—you'll love it

Laid back—relaxed and easygoing

Lay it on me—tell me

Off the wall—weird

Psychedelic—dreamy, swirly, and wild

Right on—sounds good; I approve

Square—uncool

Turn on to—start to like and understand

Unreal—so amazing it's hard to believe

Uptight—tense

Where it's at—a good place or situation

You dig?—You understand? You like it?

Vibe—feeling, atmosphere

CHAPTER 6
Saturday

Early Saturday morning, the audience woke up to a man at the stage microphone shouting, "Goood morrrning!" It was Mel Lawrence from

the Woodstock Ventures staff. The volume on his microphone had accidentally gotten turned up too loud. Immediately, heads in the audience popped up. People were groggy and a little annoyed. Lawrence apologized, lowered the volume, and began announcements. "We're going to have another groovy day," he predicted. At this, cheers sounded.

He told the audience that the outside world thought things were bad at Woodstock. But really everything was okay and they should all be proud of themselves. Joel Rosenman would later tell interviewers that it seemed like the more the outside world expected disaster, the more the fans refused to allow Woodstock to fail.

Big plastic garbage bags were passed around. The crowd helped out, stowing their trash till the bags were full. "What we have in mind is breakfast in bed for four hundred thousand," Wavy Gravy announced.

The commune served granola to the fans. For much of the crowd, it was either that or go hungry. So they ate it. Few had heard of granola back then. The festival helped make it famous.

Back home, many families were worried. Were their kids okay? The newspapers told of parked cars blocking roads for miles. Gas stations were out of gas. Even townspeople were trapped at home for the weekend. No one had cell phones in those days. There were pay phones at the festival, but not enough. Parents started calling local police or festival headquarters for news.

At least three-quarters of the people at Woodstock were between ages seventeen and twenty-three. Most had never taken care of themselves in the outdoors, away from home for a whole weekend. Some came prepared, but others didn't. They didn't bring extra clothes, tents, sleeping bags, or blankets. Some came barefoot.

Most didn't bring much food or water. Maybe they only brought a few oranges or bags of chips. Some left their supplies in their cars, thinking they could go back for them later. They didn't realize how far they had parked from the festival, though, and didn't get back till the concert was over. Fans had expected to be able to buy food and other supplies at the festival or in nearby towns. But the stores quickly ran out.

During the festival, Michael Lang went around to check on things. He rode a motorcycle and usually wore jeans and a leather vest. He worked hard

but was laid back. That meant he didn't worry too much. When his team got upset, he might tell them to relax and enjoy the music. Sometimes that was helpful, but sometimes it just meant other people would have to fix problems that he didn't.

There seemed to be a new crisis every time the festival staff turned around. By now, the portable toilets along the edge of the hill were overflowing. Trucks couldn't get in to clean or repair them. The only choice was to dig big holes and bury the stinky mess. For the rest of the festival there were long lines for the bathrooms. Toilet paper was like gold and just as hard to find. Some people got frustrated and went in the nearby woods or in the yards of Yasgur's neighbors.

People would leave their groups to use the bathroom, then couldn't find their way back again. Woodstock was so crowded that it could take hours just to walk from the back of the crowd to the stage. Since there were no ushers and no seats, it was easy to get lost. Kids looking for friends wrote messages that were read aloud by staff onstage. When this became too much, only the most urgent ones were read. Others were posted on bulletin boards or tacked to trees around the festival grounds.

Doctors and nurses treated about four thousand fans with medical problems in a tent at the bottom of the hill. Most injuries and illnesses were minor. Some fans caught colds. Lots of feet got cut from stepping on rocks by the lakes or trash in the mud. However, dangerous illegal drugs like LSD were being passed around. If someone had a bad reaction to drugs, there was a "freak out" tent. Inside, Hog Farmers tried calming them down. More serious medical cases were flown out to a hospital by helicopter.

There were two known deaths as a result of the festival. One fan died of a drug overdose at a nearby hospital. Tragedy struck again when a tractor accidentally ran over a teenager in his sleeping bag, killing him. The Woodstock team was horrified and saddened. However, most of the crowd probably didn't know until after the festival when they read about it in the news. There were rumors of a baby being born at the festival, but that may not be true. It's more likely the birth happened in festival traffic or that the mother was airlifted out of the festival to have her baby in a hospital.

Friday's rain had turned the hillside into a muddy mess. However, the audience made the best of it. Some even slipped and slid in the mud for fun. It was a hot summer weekend, and there was no place to take a shower, though some kids swam in the lakes.

If you care about staying clean and well-fed, Woodstock was not the place for you. Are you wondering why so many people in the audience stayed despite things getting kind of tough? Probably for the music and friendship. All around were people of the same age. People who understood one another and the problems they shared. People who liked rock music, long hair, and a good time. These fans knew they were in the middle of a once-in-a-lifetime event. No way were they leaving! Not yet.

Altamont

There were some troubles at the Woodstock music festival, but overall it was an upbeat weekend. However, another concert held four months later in Altamont, California, erupted in violence. It was a free one-day music event headlined by the Rolling Stones. Some of the Woodstock bands performed there, too. A motorcycle group called the Hell's Angels was hired for security. But fights broke out. Tragically, a fan was killed and there were other accidental deaths as well as injuries. The concert at Altamont was the opposite of Woodstock.

Rolling Stones

CHAPTER 7
Saturday and Sunday

Not all of the bands at Woodstock were famous. Saturday's music started at 12:15 in the afternoon with a little known jazz-rock group named Quill.

Another band named Santana was popular in California before the festival, but nowhere else. Lang and Kornfeld had just happened to hear one of their songs. They loved their Latin-rock sound and signed them. Carlos Santana was the group's leader. The band had lots of energy, playing songs like "Soul Sacrifice." Woodstock helped introduce Santana to the world. By 1970, their songs "Black Magic Woman" and "Evil Ways" would be on the charts of Billboard, a music-trend magazine that ranks songs by their sales.

Carlos Santana

More bands including Canned Heat and Mountain rocked the stage that day. Around 10:30 that night came a group many had been waiting for—the Grateful Dead. Their faithful fans sometimes call themselves Deadheads. Some

Grateful Dead

who heard them thought they were great at Woodstock. Others said they weren't as good as usual. But it wasn't the band's fault. It had rained, and the stage was wet. The Dead kept getting shocked by their electric guitars and microphones!

Next on the program, Creedence Clearwater Revival played rock-and-roll and blues songs including "Bad Moon Rising" and winding up with "Suzie Q." It was 2:00 a.m., time for the concert to end. But there were still four more groups to go!

Janis Joplin performed next. She was a mega rock-and-roll star in the sixties. She had wild long hair and wore hippie clothes and dozens of

Janis Joplin

bracelets. Her performances were usually intense and heartfelt. However, some thought she was not quite her best at Woodstock because she had to play so late that night.

Sly & the Family Stone didn't get onstage till 3:30 Sunday morning. The group had a unique funky soul sound. Even though some people were sleeping, Sly got them up and clapping with songs like "Stand!" and "Dance to the Music." He wore big rose-tinted glasses and furry white boots.

Sly & the Family Stone

The Who

Did the music end for the night after Sly? No!
A superstar British band called The Who
started at 5:00 a.m. with Roger Daltrey singing
lead. He had wild wavy hair and wore a vest
with long fringe that swayed in the darkness.

Sometimes he would sling his microphone around
on its cord. Popular guitarist Pete Townshend did
his trademark leaps in the air. At one point during
their show, an antiwar activist named Abbie
Hoffman rushed the stage. He had been a big

help in organizing the medical tent. But now he wanted to speak out to the crowd about politics. Townshend didn't recognize him and whacked him with his guitar. Hoffman leaped offstage. But he was okay and the concert continued.

Michael Lang considered The Who the high point of the day. In all, the band performed a whopping twenty-four songs including "Pinball Wizard" and "See Me, Feel Me." Their set lasted till around 6:00 a.m. Sunday morning. Wow!

Although loving the music, many fans were exhausted and falling asleep. That probably wasn't good news if you were the last band to play in the lineup. Jefferson Airplane, with lead singer Grace Slick, had waited all night for their turn to perform. They were tired, too, and nervous. But they belted out their most popular songs like "Somebody to Love" and "White Rabbit." The show ended around 10:30 Sunday morning.

Jefferson
Airplane

Earlier that day, a call for basic supplies had gone out from Woodstock Ventures headquarters. Nearby communities, churches, and hotels pitched in and gathered food to give away, including thousands of peanut butter and jelly sandwiches. Max Yasgur gave free milk and butter from his dairy, and bought bread to be passed out. In a makeshift kitchen the Hog Farm cooked thousands of simple meals such as brown rice and veggies.

And by helicopter, soldiers brought in snacks including candy bars and sodas. At one point they dropped oranges and flowers down to fans on the hill. Grateful fans shared the food and tucked the flowers in their hair.

As food grew scarce, prices were being jacked up. Instead of a quarter, hot dogs were now a dollar. That night, some food trucks at the festival were burned in protest. This was the only known act of violence at the festival. Amazing, considering how big the crowd was.

Finally, most everyone went to sleep. However, the next day would bring a different kind of trouble. Storms!

CHAPTER 8
Sunday

The music began again at two in the afternoon on Sunday. Joe Cocker was first up. He was a British singer with a growling, gritty voice. He wore striped bellbottoms, a tie-dyed shirt, and had a style all his own. When his band played, he pretended to strum an invisible guitar along with them. His body, face, and hands jerked all around. He almost seemed like he was having a fit, but this was just how he looked when he sang. And he had a powerful blues-rock sound. Fans couldn't take their eyes off him.

As he wound up his last number, "With a Little Help from My Friends," a mighty thunderstorm hit! Strong winds whipped up. Black clouds blew in fast. Lightning cracked.

Joe Cocker

People in the crowd wrapped up in blankets or tarps if they had them. They hugged each other and ducked their heads. Others shrieked and ran for cover.

As Cocker and his band dashed offstage, the crew swarmed onstage to cover or remove electrical equipment. The tarps overhead were flapping wildly. John Morris yelled at the crews to stop. The storm

was too dangerous! Soon Morris stood alone at the microphone facing the crowd. It was brave of him. He might have been electrocuted by lightning or wet power cables on the stage. But he wanted to control and calm the fans if he could. The last thing they needed was mass panic! Desperate, he got the crowd chanting over and over, "No rain, no rain." They were trying to wish the storm away. But it was no use.

One of the biggest dangers came from sound equipment towers that stood in front of Morris. They were about seventy feet tall—as high as a six-story building—and were made of yellow metal

poles and wood planks loaded with heavy speakers. They were like monkey bars, and fans had been climbing them to get a good view of the stage all during the concert. Although Morris kept begging them to get down, some were having too much fun. As the storm grew worse, however, they did as he asked. Still, the towers heaved and swayed in the wind. If they fell, fans sitting on the hill could die. That would have brought the festival to a terrible end.

Rain kept pounding for two and a half hours. It turned the hillside into ankle-deep mud. It loosened the soil, causing the stage to slide a few inches sideways. When the wind, rain, and lightning finally stopped, everyone breathed a sigh of relief. The towers stayed put. No one was hurt.

A crew began sweeping water off the stage. Around that time, Max Yasgur dropped by. Lang and Lawrence asked him to go onstage and speak to the wet fans. Yasgur wasn't used to big crowds, but he agreed.

Looking out over the audience, the dairy farmer spoke into the mike. "I think you people have proven something to the world . . . that a half a million kids . . . can get together and have three

days of fun and music . . . and I God-bless you for it!" The crowd whooped, clapped, and cheered. Max Yasgur had lifted their sagging, soggy spirits!

Unfortunately the rain had caused serious problems. Soil covering electrical cables was washed away. The cables that were for amplifiers got stepped on and were cracking open. Water was reaching the high-voltage wires inside. For a tense moment, the promoters actually considered ending the festival. They didn't want to take a chance that musicians would get fried onstage!

The question on everyone's mind was: Would the festival be cut short?

CHAPTER 9
The Last Songs

Country Joe and the Fish were supposed to play next. Despite the danger, they were eager to perform and came onstage. The microphones were off while attempts were made to repair the electricity. So the fans on the hillside couldn't hear the band. It didn't matter that much. Country Joe and the Fish simply banged pots and pans, played drums and a ukulele, and rang cowbells. They tossed canned drinks and oranges into the audience. Surprisingly, this was entertaining!

Meanwhile, electrical power was rerouted to other strong cables. Would it be enough? It was! Country Joe and the Fish went on to perform their regular songs. For now, Woodstock would continue as planned. Well-known rock groups

played—Ten Years After; The Band; musician
Johnny Winter; and Blood, Sweat & Tears.

Most fans didn't know the next band. But later,
they would be called a highlight of the festival.
They were Crosby, Stills & Nash. Neil Young,
a fourth band member, joined partway through

Neil Young with Crosby, Stills & Nash

their performance. Their songs were mellow but catchy with beautiful harmonies. At one point, Stephen Stills told the crowd, "This is the second time we've ever played in front of people, man. We're scared." He didn't need to worry. Everyone loved them!

Jimi Hendrix was the very last to play at Woodstock. Music had gone on throughout the night, and it was now 8:30 Monday morning. Hendrix must have been exhausted. Many tired fans had already gone home to jobs or school. There were only about thirty-five thousand people left. But Hendrix didn't care. He played his heart out. Those who'd left missed an amazing finale!

Most bands had played thirty- to ninety-minute music sets. But Jimi Hendrix played for two hours. He wore a bright red scarf tied around his afro and a white jacket with blue-beaded fringe.

With his white Stratocaster electric guitar he played "The Star-Spangled Banner" and stunned the audience. He turned it into a rock song! Few had ever seen that kind of playing before. In fact, some people still talk about it. He had a unique sound and blended several styles into one that was all his own. He got those tired fans on their feet.

As his last notes died away, the festival came to an end. There had been many kinds of musical styles—rock, hard rock, folk, blues, funk, jazz, Latin, Indian, and blends of all the above.

It was time for the last fans to find their cars. Some tried to help clean up the hillside mess. But it was an overwhelming chore. Sleeping bags drenched in mud were too heavy to be carried home.

Between thirty thousand and eighty thousand got left on the hillside. Everywhere, there were paper plates and bags, milk cartons, snack wrappers, and empty soda, bean, and soup cans. It looked and smelled like a trash dump.

A cleaning crew came in and walked the site. They hammered nails in the ends of long sticks and used them to pick things up. Trash was gathered into piles and hauled off in trucks. Some of the sleeping bags were cleaned and given to needy families. A local Boy Scout troop helped with the cleanup, too. Eventually, the trash was gone. The hillside was still a muddy mess. Later on, Max Yasgur was paid for the damage to his land. And lush green alfalfa grew there again.

The three-day event certainly had been a great success. But now Woodstock Ventures had to face a bitter fact. It looked like their concert had been a complete money-loser!

CHAPTER 10
Curious

Right after the festival that Monday morning, some of the musicians were taped for a guest appearance on the popular Dick Cavett TV talk show. Jefferson Airplane and others from the concert performed. They talked about the amazing time at Woodstock.

Stephen Stills from Crosby, Stills, Nash & Young showed the TV audience the mud still caked on his clothes from Yasgur's farm.

David Crosby said this about the festival: "It was incredible. It was probably the strangest thing that's ever happened in the world." He described the crowd he'd seen below as the band had flown in by helicopter to perform. He said, "It looked like an encampment of the Macedonian army on a Greek hill, crossed with the biggest batch of gypsies you ever saw."

The more they heard, the more Americans wanted to know about the festival. Reporters interviewed people from the nearby town of Bethel. Most had good things to say, even those who had worried beforehand about trouble.

When a woman dropped a shopping bag in a market, kids had helped pick up her groceries. When a state trooper's car ran off the road, fans helped push it back on. They were also spotted delivering drinks to thirsty traffic officers. It turned out that the hippies and other young music fans were mostly respectful and helpful.

Still, the festival might not have lived on in people's minds or become so famous if not for one thing. Michael Wadleigh's movie *Woodstock: Three Days of Peace and Music* came out in theaters

in 1970. The three-hour film won the Best Documentary Academy Award in 1971. It was a huge hit!

Not all the Woodstock bands made it into the movie. The crew didn't have enough film to catch everything, and sometimes their film equipment didn't work during the concert. Plus, certain bands had refused to be filmed, perhaps not realizing what great publicity it was.

Today, some people still argue about details of what happened onstage at Woodstock. Which songs did each band play, and in what order? Music fans even disagree about the lineup of the bands. There was a lot of confusion at the concert, and no official record was kept.

One thing is certain. Some bands became stars as a result of the concert and film. Those who were already stars gained many new fans. Songs such as Richie Havens's "Freedom" and Jimi Hendrix's "Star-Spangled Banner" were heard around the nation! The theme song for the film was written by Joni Mitchell and performed by Crosby, Stills, Nash & Young. It was titled "Woodstock" and helped CSNY's popularity skyrocket.

Joni Mitchell

The movie didn't just feature bands, though. Using a split-screen effect, it often displayed two or more images at the same time. While a band performed, images of the crowd appeared alongside. Finally, the curious world got to see what had gone on at the festival, onstage and off.

They got a glimpse of what hippies were really like. Highlights included young people playing in the mud, skinny-dipping, and climbing the sound towers in the storm. And grooving on the music. There was even a nun flashing a peace sign!

Woodstock Ventures lost over a million dollars on the festival. Lawsuits were filed against them for various reasons. The money owed was eventually paid off. Over time, the movie made some of those involved in the concert rich.

Was the festival a success? Max Yasgur thought so. Half a million young people had found a way to come together in music and peace. Right smack in the middle of troubled times in the United States. He thought that maybe grown-ups could learn a thing or two from those kids.

Some of the fans, law officers, musicians, and townspeople only remembered the mud and the mix-ups at Woodstock. Still, despite all the problems, there was almost no violence. Most who were there considered Woodstock a life-changing adventure. They knew they'd been part of an amazing happening. In fact, many baby boomers who didn't go to the festival were bummed out— disappointed they missed it.

There had been a feeling of togetherness and hope for the future that weekend. Strangers made friends and shared what they had. Old people and young people gained respect for one another. It had been a special moment in time. A memory they would carry with them all their lives.

And best of all, the music was far out. Woodstock is still considered one of the greatest, grooviest concerts ever!

Celebrating Woodstock

In 1984, a plaque was placed at Yasgur's farm to honor the 1969 Woodstock festival. Years later, a performing arts pavilion and museum were built there. The museum has exhibits about life in the 1960s and people and events at the festival. There's a psychedelic painted bus and Volkswagen Beetle on display, and a theater-in-the-round where scenes from the Woodstock concert are shown. The nearby hill where half a million fans sat to enjoy three days of music has been preserved. People, young and old, can visit to discover or remember the Woodstock Festival of 1969!

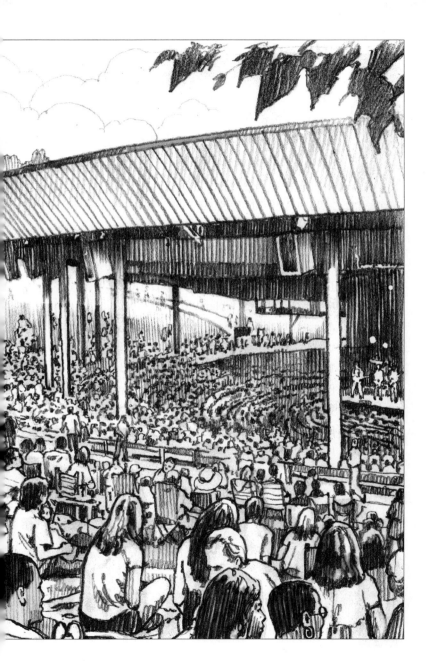

Timeline of Woodstock

1967	Monterey Pop, the first commercial outdoor rock concert in the United States, is held
1968	Michael Lang organizes the Miami Pop Festival for over twenty-five thousnad fans
	Lang and Artie Kornfeld get the idea to have an outdoor arts and music festival
Feb 1969	Lang and Kornfeld meet partners Joel Rosenman and John Roberts
July 1969	The town of Wallkill turns the festival away; Max Yasgur leases his land to the festival
Aug 13, 1969 (Wednesday)	About fifty thousand people come early to the festival
Aug 15, 1969 (Friday)	The festival is declared open with free admission
	Richie Havens is the first musician to play at the Woodstock Festival
Aug 16-17, 1969 (Saturday to Sunday)	Bands include Crosby, Stills, Nash & Young; Santana; Janis Joplin; Grateful Dead; and The Who
	A thunderstorm hits on Sunday
Aug 18, 1969 (Monday)	Jimi Hendrix is the last musician to play at the festival
1970	Woodstock documentary film premiers
1994	25th anniversary Woodstock concert held in Saugerties, New York
1999	30th anniversary Woodstock concert held in Rome, New York

Timeline of the World

1961	Germany's Berlin Wall is built
1962	Andy Warhol's *Soup Cans* goes on display
	The first Walmart opens
1963	President John F. Kennedy is assassinated
	Dr. Martin Luther King Jr. makes his "I Have a Dream" speech
1964	Hasbro sells first GI Joe action figures
1965	President Lyndon Johnson sends ground troops into Vietnam
1966	Chinese leader Mao Zedong starts the Cultural Revolution
	National Organization for Women (NOW) founded
	Star Trek TV series begins
1967	First football Super Bowl
1968	Martin Luther King Jr. and Robert F. Kennedy are assassinated
	Construction begins on the first World Trade Center tower in New York
1969	Neil Armstrong is the first man to walk on the moon
	Hurricane Camille kills approximately 250 people in the United States
	Beatle John Lennon marries Yoko Ono
1970	In Ohio, four Kent State University students protesting the Vietnam War are shot and killed by National Guard troops
1973	Last US combat troops leave Vietnam
1975	South Vietnam falls to North Vietnamese communists

Here is a list of some children's books that will tell you more about the 1960s.

Caputo, Philip. *10,000 Days of Thunder: A History of the Vietnam War*. New York: Atheneum, 2005.

Krull, Kathleen. *What Was the March on Washington?* New York: Grosset & Dunlap, 2013.

Murray, Stuart. *Vietnam War*. New York: DK, 2005.

O'Connor, Jim. *Who Is Bob Dylan?* New York: Grosset & Dunlap, 2013.

Partridge, Elizabeth. *John Lennon: All I Want Is the Truth*. New York: Viking, 2005.

Partridge, Elizabeth. *Marching for Freedom: Walk Together, Children, and Don't You Grow Weary*. New York: Viking, 2009.

Woodstock producers Joel Rosenman and John Roberts

Michael Lang (left) and Chip Monck (right)

Traffic jam on the road to Woodstock

A campsite at Woodstock

A festivalgoer taking a break

A festivalgoer leaps into a pile of hay

Famous Woodstock movie poster

Volunteers making food for the crowd

Country Joe & The Fish perform

Aerial view of the crowd

Richie Havens performs to a massive crowd

A couple greets the dawn among festivalgoers

Janis Joplin performing late into the night

The Who perform before dawn on Sunday

Left to right: John Entwistle, Roger Daltrey, Keith Moon, and Pete Townshend

Jimi Hendrix closes out the concert early Monday morning

Festivalgoers climbing the sound towers

Max and Miriam Yasgur after the festival